RAISING A
Prodigal
A STORY OF ENCOURAGEMENT

MARSHA MCLEAN

Studio Griffin
A Publishing Company
www.studiogriffin.net

Raising A Prodigal. A Story of Encouragement. Copyright © 2020 Marsha McLean

All Rights Reserved. Printed in the United States of America.

No part of this book may be used or reproduced in any manner whatsoever without written permission except in the case of brief quotations embodied in critical articles and reviews.

For information, contact:
Studio Griffin
A Publishing Company
Garner, North Carolina
studiogriffin@outlook.com
www.studiogriffin.net

Cover Design by Ruth E. Griffin
Image by © vlntn

First Edition

ISBN-13: 978-1-7351353-7-3

Library of Congress Control Number: 2020916701

1 2 3 4 5 6 7 8 9 10

This book is dedicated to my parents, Charles and Sabra McLean. Despite all we have been through together, I recognize that I would not be here today had it not been for the both of you.

To my son Tyrrell, thank you for being my most precious gift. I love you with a special love and there is absolutely nothing you can do about it!

To every person battling with a prodigal, this book is also dedicated to you. You will make it to the other side and brighter days await you.

TABLE OF CONTENTS

Introduction	1
Chapter One	4
Chapter Two	6
Chapter Three	8
Chapter Four	10
Chapter Five	11
Chapter Six	13
Chapter Seven	15
Chapter Eight	17
Chapter Nine	19
Chapter Ten	21
Chapter Eleven	23
Chapter Twelve	26
Chapter Thirteen	28
Chapter Fourteen	31
Chapter Fifteen	34
Chapter Sixteen	36
Chapter Seventeen	39
Chapter Eighteen	42
Chapter Nineteen	45
Chapter Twenty	47
Afterword	51
Citations	53
Further Discussion	55
About the Author	59

RAISING A
Prodigal
A STORY OF ENCOURAGEMENT

Introduction

The Prodigal Son (Luke 15:11-32) is my favorite Bible story. In it, a rich young man leaves home, squanders his money, and ends up working as a servant. He eventually comes to himself and decides to go home, where he finds his father has been waiting for him, ready to embrace him and welcome him home.

This story is a great reminder that you can come home to get revived, start again and be successful, regardless of what you've been through. As a Licensed Clinical Mental Health Counselor and Licensed Clinical Addiction Specialist, the story of the Prodigal Son is a source of inspiration for me as I work with and help others who struggle with parenting issues, encouraging them and given them tools to help them maintain a healthy relationship with their child. As a mom, though, this story is a deeply personal one, because of my own relationship with my son. I struggled with him for many years as he challenged my parenting when he was growing up, leaving us both stressed out and overwhelmed.

That's why I decided to share my story and write this book, not just as a mother of a prodigal, but a prodigal as well, because what I've discovered is that these types of behaviors are generational. My parents were teen parents and there was a lot of abuse and lack of appreciation that came from that type of background. When you're not prepared to parent, the only thing you can do is repeat what was done. I tried to parent the way I thought was beneficial, taking the best things from my childhood for my son, but I didn't know anything about dealing with my own failure when I was struggling. So I didn't know how to help my son when he was struggling. Making your child respect you doesn't work in this day and age. I had to be creative and find what was going to work for him and for me. But I didn't have anything else. I didn't have family to get positive answers from. That's when I turned to God.

I wasn't raised in church. I didn't know anything except Easter or Christmas. But I was told about God at age eighteen or nineteen and eventually found that He'll give you a peace that no one else understands. I could go to Him in prayer and He would help me be a better parent. He wouldn't let me parent the way I was parented; instead, He would show me what to do. My faith carried me through some trying times.

Whether you're a Christian, or a person of different faith, the message of this book is the same: don't give up on your child. It's okay to feel like a failure sometimes, but don't let that stop you. Everyone makes mistakes: learn how to be prepared for the consequences. Stick in there regardless of what the situation looks like. And cultivate some confidence. You aren't alone in this.

My son is my legacy. He's going through his own issues right now, and I want him to be successful, but not necessarily the way everyone defines success: I want my son to know Christ and have confidence. And I believe, like the Prodigal Son, one day he will come home, and I'll be waiting for him with open arms.

Chapter One

If you look up the name Marsha, you will discover that it carries two meanings: 'Devoted to God' and 'War-like.' Ironically, that has been the story of my life: even in the midst of war in my life, I have remained devoted to God. I'm not sure why my mom and dad named me Marsha but as I look back on my life now, the name was prophetic. God knew even when they didn't.

As with most families, my parents, Charles and Sabra Mclean, were over the moon the day I was born. Although I was their second child, I was the first one born to them into a non-chaotic world. You see, my older sister was born when my mom and dad were sixteen and nineteen and much like most black people in the South, they were forced to get married the day they told their parents they were expecting. I can imagine how hard that was because they were babies having a baby and getting married, but they had no choice. They did the best they could and now three years later here I was crying in my mother's arms. Having me was their second chance at redemption. It was the chance to do the things right that they had done wrong with my sister. It was almost as if I was their new beginning.

But it didn't stay that way.

Chapter Two

On any given weekday, driving by Charles and Sabra's house one would think they were living the American dream. They both worked to provide for their families, had two beautiful children and most of all, it appeared they were madly in love. But as the saying goes, "If the grass looks greener on the other side, it might be AstroTurf" and in our case, that's exactly what it was. The grass was always cut on the outside but on the inside World War III was brewing.

My father was a dedicated provider on most days, but he barely talked when he was home. In fact, he talked more on the weekend with a Budweiser in his hand than he did on a Wednesday without it. He relied on that drink more and more and eventually grew addicted. It wasn't easy to watch so most times my sister and I retreated to our own worlds, much like my mother did.

As a child, I didn't know a lot about my mom, but I knew she loved our family immensely. Her love was why she dealt with not just my dad's alcoholism, but with his eventual cheating as well. She saw the best in him during a time that I don't even think he saw the best in himself. My mom was truly my dad's biggest cheerleader.

She was also his biggest enabler. It was incredible to me that I could see that, and she couldn't. Weekend after weekend, my mom would beg my dad to either stop drinking or get help; and despite her pleas he never did. This went on for years and nothing ever changed. But that's the crazy thing about my parent's relationship, they were both addicts. My dad was addicted to alcohol and my mom was addicted to loving him and the pain he caused.

Chapter Three

Bam! That was the sound of my mother's cocoa-buttered hand as it collided with my face. As much as it hurt, her slapping me didn't bother me emotionally because it wasn't the first time she had put her hands on me. It was, however, the first time I felt grown enough to tell her she needed to divorce my dad. I was sick and tired of watching her be sick and tired, so I had to speak up.

She made me regret that decision almost immediately. I don't know if my mom was mad that I told her to leave or mad at herself that she hadn't. Whatever the case was, that day was a turning point for us all. My mom started having her own affair and eventually got the nerve to pick up and divorce my dad.

Finally, a dream come true, I thought to myself. I could have peace and joy; and could get a true taste of reality. I quickly discovered that while divorce sounded and felt good to my depressed and tired mom, it turned out to be one of the worst things that had ever happened to me.

Chapter Four

My mom has always been one of those people where when she's all in, she's all in. So her relationship with her new man was no different. She loved him with every fiber of her being. But he distanced her children and caused her to do the same. To this day, I don't know how my mom went from being with a man who only acknowledged our presence on his sober days to a man who ignored our existence daily. My parents' divorce was not what I imagined it to be. And to make things worse, my mom had the bold idea to move me out of her house into my own place at the age of sixteen. Yes, I was still a baby, but much like when she got married, I was now being pushed out. Looking back, the situation made sense. If she could survive, I could survive and so suddenly her second chance at parenting turned into a recycling of generational patterns.

Chapter Five

When I was first given the keys to my own apartment, I couldn't believe it. In fact, it still feels like a dream when I think about it. Some days though, I must admit it was more of a nightmare, but a dream, nonetheless.

As the thought and reality of being "alone" sank in, I quickly discovered that living on my own was an experience I never expected it to be. I was ecstatic to have newfound freedom, but I was also a terrified little girl. I did not know anything about being an adult and being kicked out of my mother's home as a child didn't help anybody, especially me.

Prior to my teenage years, I loved being at home with my parents. Despite the constant arguing that occurred in our home, home still felt like my safe place. It was the place I went to when I wanted to get lost in a book or in my journal. I was sheltered but being sheltered didn't bother me as long as I felt safe. But I lost that safety the day I moved out on my own.

After just a few months of living on my own, I decided to take my life into my own hands. I started hanging out at local bars and clubs and before I knew it, I was becoming a target for older men. I had it all: intelligence, curves, naivety, a place of my own and no overbearing parents. I was truly the perfect candidate for R. Kelly before there was an R. Kelly.

Chapter Six

"What is your name?" he asked me.

I still remember the day I met the man I thought I would be with forever. He was seven years my senior and was everything I imagined in a man. I'm sure I was everything he imagined in a young girl to prey on.

We would hang out, have sex, hang out and have sex again; and before I knew it I was barely attending school. I knew my parents saw my life spiraling downward; however, my mom was so consumed with her own life and my dad with alcohol that neither of them ever took the time to really check on me. They didn't care about saving my life, they couldn't even save their own. I'm sure it was devastating from the outside looking in and honestly now that I'm an adult, I think a lot of my behavior was a cry for help. I needed someone to love me. I needed someone to care. Most of all, I needed someone to call the police on my boyfriend and force our relationship to end; and sadly, none of those things happened.

I'm sure he didn't really love me, but he made me feel like he did. But I would only see him at certain times of the day before he would go run back to his mother's house. It all felt a little backwards to me. I should have been the one running to my mom's house yet here I was, a child living the life of an adult.

Chapter Seven

When I was a little girl, I always found my greatest escape in books. They offered the opportunity to become someone else for a limited amount of time without the fear of being judged. It was also the only time I could truly be 'Marsha', the innocent little girl everyone else loved to be around. There are still days that I look back and long for that Marsha because I often feel as if her innocence was taken too soon.

You see, when my boyfriend took my virginity at sixteen, I had no idea what I was doing. He convinced me to give him my most prized possession and even though I didn't feel like I was ready, he convinced me that I was. For months, I wondered if this is what real love felt like and over time I realized that if I had to question it, it was a harsh reminder that it probably was not.

Positive? What does positive mean? It means I'm positively not pregnant right? It has to mean that because there's no way I could be pregnant!

This is what I thought to myself as I sat looking at the results of the pregnancy test that I had just taken. Me, a seventeen-year-old fast food worker was pregnant with what I would soon discover to be my son. I still remember the day like it was yesterday because that was the day I truly lost my innocence.

Great, this is exactly what I need, I thought to myself sarcastically. A baby with a man seven years my senior who still lived with his mom.

I couldn't believe this was happening to me. I wasn't being irresponsible. In fact, I was on birth control faithfully and yet here I was, pregnant by a man who had just fathered a child prior to meeting me. I knew he was not a good father. I saw his lack of fathering skills with his last child and I knew that if he wasn't a good father to the one he had, he wasn't going to be a good father to the child we had on the way. And not only that, but he was far from the model boyfriend. He was regularly abusing me, mentally and physically and I stayed because I didn't know what else to do. I was stuck. Not only was I seventeen, but I was four months pregnant which meant even if I considered an abortion, it wasn't an option.

Chapter Eight

For weeks after finding out the news, I had trouble believing that I would be giving birth to a baby boy. I had sunk into a whirlwind of depression that no amount of medication could pull me out of it. Getting out of bed became a chore and crying to my sleep became the norm. "What had I gotten myself into?" was the question I often asked myself when I was in the presence of my boyfriend. This was not the life I had signed up for, but if I didn't sign up for it, then who in the world did?

When I first got the news that I would be giving birth to my son, I didn't know who to tell but I knew I needed to tell someone. At the time, I was not really excited about becoming a mom and I knew deep down if I wasn't excited, no one else would be either. You see, there was no way my baby would be special to anyone else other than me because my sister already had kids. And now I was pregnant by a man who had fathered a child with another woman. Nobody would care, or so I thought.

I still remember like it was yesterday, when I looked at my sister and saw the joy in her eyes when I told her that I would be giving birth to her first nephew.

"Oh my God, this is great," she exclaimed to my surprise. I was amazed that she would be so supportive. Whose sister was this? I thought to myself. Surely, this wasn't my sister being supportive. She had never supported anybody other than herself and suddenly she was happy for me? Yeah right. I didn't know if I should be sick or mortified by her response but at the time I kind of went with it.

"I'm so happy you're pregnant so now I'm not the only screw-up in the family," she said.

Wow.

Chapter Nine

This is what support looked like for my family, supporting that she wasn't the only screw up.

My sister's support (or lack thereof) wasn't the only thing that I was fighting against. In fact, not only was I four months pregnant but I also had five months until I officially graduated from high school and the pressure to graduate and perform well intensified.

Don't get me wrong, I was never a dummy but between the drama my boyfriend brought to the table and my now pregnant belly protruding in front of me everywhere I went, life was challenging. I was terrified.

But I was also committed to doing everything possible to ensure I graduated on time. Sure, my boyfriend was always in the background telling me I didn't need to finish school, but I didn't need my son growing up with two high-school dropout parents. There was no way I was going to allow that to happen. My life became about my unborn child and I was determined to do everything I could to set the bar high for him. He was never going to worry about becoming the man his father was, if I had any say about it.

Chapter Ten

"I think I'm going into labor," I told my boyfriend one night just a few weeks shy of my high school graduation. It was a dark night and I had no real idea of what was going on. As sweat dripped down my face and my heart raced faster than a black man trying to escape a Scary Movie scene, I knew something wasn't right.

"Lord, please take me now," I silently prayed to myself that night as we drove to the hospital. I wasn't a praying woman at that time, but I knew that I had always heard that God would answer my prayers; and in that moment, I needed to die. I wasn't ready to become a mom and I surely wasn't ready to experience life as a parent alongside a boyfriend I still struggled to engage with on a consistent and non-dramatic basis.

But I didn't die that night and looking back at it now, it is the one time in my life I can truly say I thank God for not answering prayers. As I held my baby boy in my arms, thinking of my relationship with his father, I couldn't help but wonder if giving birth would finally make him love me the way I desired to be loved. I believed that this was my opportunity to finally turn the page and so naming my son after his father despite the abuse and pain he put me through sounded like a good idea.

"I'm going to name him after you," I said gushing at him and my newborn baby.

"Really?" he asked with a smile on his face.

"Yes, really," I said smiling back; and in that moment despite everything we had gone through together, my son's father knew he had me and his newborn son now wrapped around his little finger.

Chapter Eleven

The first four months of motherhood were tumultuous, to say the least. I knew prior to giving birth to my son that support would be something that wouldn't come easy to me; however, I never expected it to be as hard as it was. In fact, as a new mom, I had to keep my head above water the best way I knew how and for me that was by filing for welfare. In those days, I didn't care what people thought about me or my decisions. I was a teenager and had to do what I needed to do to make sure that my child was taken care of and if that meant I had to be on welfare then welfare it was. I wasn't too proud to get help when I needed it the most.

While getting money was never an issue for me, the one thing that was an issue was my boyfriend and his hands. I was dating an abuser. He was beating me practically every day. But now that I had a son, I knew I had to change that. It took some time but eventually I made the decision that enough was enough, and I called the police. He was arrested immediately and suddenly I felt a sense of relief.

Finally, I thought to myself. After years of abuse, I was finally free, and I would be able to live the life I thought my son and I deserved.

Then my mom called.

"Drop the charges," she said to me.

"Excuse me? This man just beat me," I said trying to make sense of the bombshell that she dropped on me.

"I know he did but as your mom I am asking you to drop the charges."

I went completely silent and the only thing that could be heard was the heavy breathing happening between us.

"Marsha, are you there?"

"Yes."

"Drop the charges, your son needs his dad," she offered as an explanation.

"Ok," I said.

Later that day, I dropped the charges and within hours, it became one of the worst decisions of my life.

Chapter Twelve

"I'm going to kill you," my boyfriend said to me as he glared at me with piercing and angered eyes.

Was I dreaming? This couldn't be real right? Could the man I had just had a baby with be really standing over me threatening to kill me? I asked myself.

"Where's my baby?" I demanded as I fought back the tears beginning to form in my eyes.

"He's sleep," he said as he began to take my clothes off and sexually assault me. I'm really about to die, I thought to myself, but something stirred up in me and I knew that if I was going to die, I was going to die fighting. I pushed him off me and made a sprint to go pick up my baby. I didn't care how risky running felt, it was my only option. My boyfriend was mortified but I didn't care as I ran out of the door with my baby in hand to the nearest neighbor's home to call 911.

"My boyfriend just broke into my home and tried to kill me, and I need help!" I yelled at the other end of the line. Within minutes, the police had arrived at my home and arrested him, again. As I sat on the doorsteps watching the life with my abuser end for good this time, I couldn't help but stop shaking. I couldn't believe that my mom had convinced me to drop the charges. He could have easily killed me and my son and then what? Would my mother have even cared? There were so many questions that I had but if I didn't know anything else I knew one thing, I was done with him.

Chapter Thirteen

Leaving my boyfriend was a pivotal move for me. Unfortunately, it wasn't the end of my problems. In fact, in many ways, leaving him behind was only the beginning of much harsher times in my life. After he had tried to kill me, I immediately pressed charges. Most women would have commended me for that but my mother, my own flesh and blood, encouraged me to drop the charges again. I didn't understand then and I sure don't understand now, but my mother was convinced that my son needed his father in his life and that if I opted to press charges I was assuring they would never have a relationship. At this point, I didn't care about a relationship with him but my mother did and so I decided to drop the charges, again.

Despite the dropped charges, I never did go back to my boyfriend. I left him behind and moved on with my life. I also changed my son's name to Tyrrell. I didn't want the daily reminder of his father in my life. And I didn't want him tagged with the name of an abuser.

Raising A Prodigal

It was during this time that I met my guardian angel, Sheila Winston. When I first met her I wasn't completely sure how well the two of us would mesh together; however, she quickly proved me wrong. Her love for God radiated through her and for someone like me who was lost without true direction, having her in my life is what gave me the strength to keep moving forward.

In many ways, she became a second mother to me. She was a positive role-model and inspired me to further my education, work harder and most of all, be a woman who pursued God wholeheartedly. As much as I love God now, I didn't really have a strong understanding of Him during the formative days in my life. In fact, I think I questioned God more than I praised Him.

Why was I in an abusive relationship? Why did my dad leave us? Why did my mother choose her boyfriend over me?

I had so many questions for God, but as I deepened my relationship with Him, I quickly discovered that just like the prophet Jeremiah in the Bible, God knew the plans He had for me (Jeremiah 29:11-13). I didn't understand the plan then but as time progressed, I slowly started to see that God really did have His best in mind for me.

Chapter Fourteen

"God, why is this happening to me?" is the question I asked myself repeatedly as I did practically everything with my son in my arms.

Go to the laundromat—together.

Wash dishes—together.

Do homework—together.

Go to church—together.

You name it and I can assure you that we did it together. But in spite of everything we did do, there was one thing we did separately and that was go to school. You see, there's this rule in parenting that says the one time you have to separate from your child is when they go to school and while it can feel like a few hours of freedom to you, it can secretly be a prison for your child.

My son was a great kid, but he faced a variety of challenges early in his school career that I wish I could have helped him avoid. Couple that with being a black boy and you have a whole new set of problems.

Even as I celebrated his arrival, the reality that I was bringing a black boy into a world that historically hates black boys stayed in the back of my mind. I couldn't stop thinking about all of the boys who never got a chance to be men because of their perceived threat on society. Trayvon Martin, Mike Brown, Emmet Till and countless of other young boys, whose lives were cut short because they were "scary." Or because their music was too loud. Or because someone felt like they didn't belong, but really, because they were black.

Is it any wonder that I was afraid to let my son out of my sight? This society fears black boys and that scared the hell out of me. This wasn't just me being a dramatic mom, either. Actual research studies show that black people are perceived to be less innocent than whites and other people. In general, Black children are rated as being significantly less innocent than white people, period. Phillip Goff, the researcher behind the study, sums it up by saying, "Our research found that black boys can be seen as responsible for their actions at an age when white boys still benefit from the assumption that children are essentially innocent." (1)

Believe it or not, my fear was justified and all I ever wanted was to protect my son from the world that inevitably awaited him.

Chapter Fifteen

"Mommy, they've been picking on me."

These were the words that came out of my son's mouth daily during his early years of school. As my heart sank into my stomach, I waited patiently as my son described to me the turmoil he was experiencing in school. On one hand, I was extremely upset that my son was subjected to such heartbreaking bullying; yet on the other hand, I was absolutely flabbergasted that my son's teacher was idly sitting back and watching other children tear him down without ever taking the time to intervene.

"Son, it's okay," I told him one day and then attempted to convince him that this latest incident of bullying would never happen again.

"I don't want to go back to school," he said to me and then looked me deep in my eyes with a look that even I couldn't break away from.

"Well baby, that's not an option," I said to him still attempting to console him.

"I don't like it," he said; and despite his hate for his school, I knew there was little that I could do to get him away, especially as a single mom.

As I take a moment to reflect on that first time my son told me about the bullying, I often beat myself up because maybe I could have said something more to encourage him. Or talked more to his teacher or to the moms of the children picking on him. Instead, I just consoled him. If I done a little more, things might have turned out differently for him; or he would have still turned out to hate school regardless of what I did and not do. Outcome aside, this one bullying instance early on soon turned out to set the precedent for the remainder of his time in school.

Chapter Sixteen

As a mom, my number one goal has always been to protect my son and to make sure that I taught him everything I knew at a young age. When the bullying began, I felt like I had done him a disservice, but when I noticed him beginning to struggle in grade school, my heart broke so much more. You see as a mom, I wrongfully expected that when I dropped my son off at school every day that he would be in good hands. I thought that his teachers and superiors would hold and treasure him as much as I did. But the reality was much different. Beginning around first grade, I began getting calls about my son's behavior as well as his inability to perform in his school work. I became alarmed.

What's going on?

Is it my son?

Is it poor parenting?

Is my son suffering because his father isn't present?

The list grew as things piled up in my brain, making me feel more and more inadequate as time went on. Then I realized trying to assign blame wasn't going to fix my problem. A couple of weeks later, as I attempted to dig into the issues that could be plaguing my son, I received a call from his school that hurt me to my core.

"Your son has Attention Deficit Disorder," they said to me.

I refused to believe it and now that I'm a trained counselor, I'm glad I refuted their initial diagnosis. Most school counselors don't have the capability to diagnose mental health issues. Being the mother that I am, I sought out some of the best mental health professionals in the world to have my son tested. It was from a credible healthcare provider that I received confirmation my son did, in fact, have Attention Deficit Disorder (ADD).

What? Not my baby, I said to myself. There was no way that my son had ADD, right?

But, according to the doctor, I was wrong. In that moment, my life was flipped upside down and the sweet child I once knew was now a child being put on medication for his behavior. In all honesty, I believe that during this time is when I began to see my relationship with my son shift in unprecedented ways. In hindsight, I wish I hadn't put him on medication so soon because a part of me feels like it made his problems worse. Instead of him being the active boy I knew him to be, he quickly turned into a zombie; and as a mom watching that progression was heart-breaking. What's even more heart-breaking is that studies have shown that black kids are diagnosed with Attention Deficit Disorder / Attention Deficit Hyper Disorder (ADHD) at a rate much quicker than any other race in our country. In addition, only thirty-six percent of black kids and thirty percent of Latino kids who had been diagnosed with ADHD were taking medication, compared to sixty-five percent of white children. (2)

Despite the struggle I had with his diagnosis, I encouraged him to take his medicine and soon I discovered that encouraging him to take medication was also pushing him into a world of deception I never expected.

Chapter Seventeen

Deception is defined as an untrue falsehood, the act of lying to or tricking someone. An example of deception is when you tell someone you are thirty when really you are forty. While I wish my son would have engaged in something as innocent as lying about his age, his deception with me started earlier than I would have ever imagined.

Around the second year of being on medication, I began to notice that my son seemed like he was getting worse and not better. In fact, there were days that I wondered if he struggled with multiple mental illnesses versus just ADD. His anger was boiling at alarming rates and as a mother trying to juggle work, school, and frequent trips to his principal's office, I just didn't feel like I had a strong grasp of things. What made this even more challenging was the lack of support that I received from his teachers. They were willing to dismiss him quickly and put him into remedial programs. My son hated me for that and there were days where I hated myself for doing it.

For quite some time, my son was on medication for his ADD and I was convinced that if his teachers wanted him to do better, they would fight this battle with me. After seeing his behavior decline and hearing his complaints about how he hated to take his medicine, I decided to do my own investigation. Sure, I knew the medication didn't make him feel like himself, but I was shocked to discover that my baby had been completely deceiving me and hadn't been taken his medicine at all. As a mom, I didn't understand how my child would stop doing anything that didn't make him feel good on the inside but now as a certified mental health specialist I know exactly why he stopped taking his medication. He felt he could manage the ADD on his own. For some, it's possible but my son wasn't one of those cases.

Had I really created an atmosphere in my home that made him feel like he couldn't talk to me openly about how he was feeling? Did he really believe that the only way he could experience freedom in his mind was to lie to me?

Raising A Prodigal

To this day, I still don't have the answer to any of those questions; however, I do know that this early sign of deception was just the beginning of even greater deception that awaited me as my son got older. Over the next several years, I would be physically and mentally deterred, but through it all I somehow managed to continue to trust in God because I knew that if I could not trust in my Lord and Savior, there was no way I would ever be able to trust anything or anyone else.

Chapter Eighteen

"Ms. Mclean you are under arrest," said the police patiently outside my door, awaiting to arrest me.

"Excuse me?" I asked, startled.

After the many years of parenting my son the best way I could, I had no reason to believe that I of all people deserved to be arrested. I worked as hard as I could every single day of my life to take care of my son. I made sure he had food on the table, clothes on his back and shoes on his feet. Yet somehow, after all the right I had done, I was still now being faced with my biggest fear, the police.

"We were told that you refused to let your son in your home," the police said to me as if him telling me what I already knew would make me let my son back into my home.

"Well, ok," I said as I went back into my home to get dressed before getting arrested. If I was going to be arrested for protecting myself from my now teenage son, then I was going to have to spend some time in jail.

Now before you can judge me and my parenting skills, I have to explain to you that things had gotten bad in my home. Not only was my son no longer following the rules of the house, but he was hanging out with groups of people I didn't agree with. He often threatened me and worst of all, he had begun spending time with his "other family". My son had begun spending time with his father and his father's family and they had convinced him that I was some sort of wild villain.

Was I a strict parent? Yes. Was I a wild villain? Absolutely not.

You see, my son learned early on how to stack the odds against me. He disrespected me day after day and when I finally drew the line in the sand, suddenly he became the victim.

Do I point the blame at my son at this age? Not really. I do however point the blame at every single person who enabled him in his chaotic behavior that ultimately put a block in our relationship. While I was hurt that the police had been called on me for enforcing tough love on my son, I lifted my head, hoping and praying that my act of love would somehow change the dangerous trajectory of my son's life.

Chapter Nineteen

Despite having the police called on me, despite the constant ridicule and bullying, I made a conscious decision as a mom to love my son anyway and opened the door for him to return home with me. As a mom, I really did love my son and so desperately wanted our relationship to work. I did everything I could to ensure it would but some days it still didn't feel like enough. At one point during our tumultuous relationship, I allowed him to live with his father but even that didn't seem to work things out in my favor.

As I began to take even more time to reflect, I realized that the quote, "If you love something, let it go," was going to have to be a quote that I lived by; and as much as it hurt, I swallowed my pride and I let my son go. Emotionally and physically. I remember friends and family often asked me if it was hard to let my son go and quite frankly it was devastating. It's almost as if you're forced to grieve the death of a life you prayed and hoped you and your child would have. It was heartbreaking, but I knew I had to let go in order for God to truly step in. I couldn't fix me and my son at the same time, so I had to make the decision to fix me first.

Fixing me first has been no easy journey, but I have learned a lot. I have learned to be a more present grandmother for my grandson, I have learned to forgive my mother and father for my own tumultuous childhood. Most of all though, I was able to go back to school to become a distinguished and sought-after Mental Health and Addiction Consultant. I have now developed a strong passion to help anyone who is in need of empowerment and self-love; and it's all because I decided to stop pointing my finger at my son and started pointing the finger at myself. I knew I couldn't expect anyone else to be better until I first became better for myself.

Chapter Twenty

As you can tell from this book, the story of the Prodigal Son is still one of my favorite stories in the Bible. Unlike the story though, it doesn't have a happily ever after ending. To date, my son and I are still not on speaking terms; however, I continue to believe by faith that one day, just like the Prodigal Son, he will find his way home.

I'm not sure who you are or what made you decide to read this book, but I am assuming it is because you have a prodigal in your own life. Maybe it's your son, your daughter, grandchild or even your spouse but, whatever the case may be, I hope you are encouraged to know that you are not alone.

As people of faith, we will all go through trying times; and even though you may not understand why you're estranged from your loved one, have comfort knowing that God hears every one of your prayers and that even if He doesn't bring your loved one to Christ today, one day He will.

I once heard a wise man say that we're all in the lives of others for a reason. To plant, to water or to reap. Maybe your job was to plant, maybe your job was to water but at the end of the day your loved one will reap all the good you have invested into them. Be not dismayed, your prodigal will come home.

Raising A Prodigal

Marsha Mclean

Afterword

If you or someone you know is having a difficult time with their child, spouse or any other family member, help is available at NAMI and SAMHSA.

NAMI National Helpline, 1-800-950-NAMI (6264), www.nami.org/About-NAMI, free service Monday - Friday, from 10am to 6pm (EST). For Help in a Crisis, Text Crisis to 741741. NAMI envisions a world where all people affected by mental illness live healthy, fulfilling lives supported by a community that cares. NAMI provides advocacy, education, support, and public awareness so that all individuals and families affected by mental illness can build better lives. NAMI Values are:

- Hope: We believe in the possibility of recovery, wellness, and the potential in all of us.
- Inclusion: We embrace diverse backgrounds, cultures, and perspectives.

- Empowerment: We promote confidence, self-efficacy, and service to our mission.
- Compassion: We practice respect, kindness, and empathy.
- Fairness: We fight for equity and justice.

SAMHSA's National Helpline, 1-800-662-HELP (4357), https://www.samhsa.gov or TTY: 1-800- 487-4889 is a confidential, free, 24-hour-a-day, 365-day-a-year, information service, in English and Spanish, for individuals and family members facing mental and/or substance use disorders. This service provides referrals to local treatment facilities, support groups, and community- based organizations. Callers can also order free publications and other information. SAMHSA's is also known as the Treatment Referral Routing Services.

If you have health insurance, you are encouraged to contact your insurer for a list of participating mental health and substance abuse providers.

For assistance with addiction, contact the National Drug Help Line at 1-844-289-0879.

Citations

1. Goff, PhD., Philip Atiba. Black Boys Viewed as Older, Less Innocent Than Whites, Research Finds. https://www.apa.org/news/press/releases/2014/03/black-boys-older. Date created: 2014

2. Frye, Devon. Children Left Behind. https://www.additudemag.com/race-and-adhd-how-people-of-color-get-left-behind/. Updated on June 18, 2020.

Marsha Mclean

Further Discussion

- Sometimes we often forget how choices will affect the next generation after us. What are some things you can do now to help the next generation?

- Hurt people, hurt people. Many times people that are raised in unhealthy homes can only give what they have witnessed. Parents often are unaware of how their upbringing may have impacted them until they have children and unfortunately, by then it is too late. What can you do today to undo some of the pain you experienced in your childhood? What are you doing to ensure your pain doesn't trickle into your own parenting?

- Many times unstable parents will make poor decisions based on their own personal struggle. What do you think your parents could have done differently?

- A bond between a mother and child is precious. That bond should be nourished at all cost. How do you keep a balance between protection and over protection? When do you seek help for excessive fear and paranoia?

- If your child is having a hard time in school such as bullying or educational struggles, you can seek support for your child. Many schools have social workers and counselors that can help you with resources for your child. You can also request testing and be provided reasonable accommodations.

- Lying is a greater significance as children enter adolescence because the child is doing it consciously, with full knowledge of the consequences. This is not the time to panic. Instead, take it as a signal to talk to your child about what's going on in their life.

- "Fixing yourself" is one of the most important steps in self-discovery and healing. What are you doing today to make sure you're personally healing?

Raising A Prodigal

Marsha Mclean

About The Author

Marsha C. Mclean is a Licensed Clinical Mental Health Counselor, Licensed Clinical Addiction Specialist, National Speaker, TV Consultant and Author. Marsha has over twenty years of experience in the Mental

Health Field. Due to her years of experience and being respected in her field, she helps train new clinicians who reside in North Carolina and Virginia. She has worked in various Human Services Organizations such as NC Department of Corrections, nonprofit organizations, and crisis services. Marsha has worked extensively with the US Military and worked briefly at the US Marine Corp Headquarters as a subject matter expert in the Substance Abuse Program Division. Marsha currently works with a diverse population in her private practice, Revive Therapeutic Services, PLLC.

Raising A Prodigal

Marsha Mclean

www.ingramcontent.com/pod-product-compliance
Lightning Source LLC
Chambersburg PA
CBHW071033080526
44587CB00015B/2592